Scotty & Friends

5 Easy Quilts
with 'Jelly Roll' 2½" Strips and 'Layer Cake' 10"x 10" Squares

'Quilt of the Month'

Quilts are not just blankets made to toss over the sofa to match the decor. Quilts embody memories, capture moments and bring comfort into our homes. They move with us from bed to bed as we grow, and travel with us when we leave home.

Quilts age into treasured heirlooms, and are passed down for generations connecting us to the loving hands of the maker, weaving stories of the past with our present lives.

The quilts we love most are the ones that get dragged about the house from beds to family room sofas. We take them outside for stargazing and sit on them while we build sandcastles on the beach. They are made in our favorite colors with motifs that are personally meaningful.

Now, you can make quilts that pack the same emotional power into each stitch. Whimsy, and warmth with a homespun attitude emanate from these simple designs.

No matter what colors you choose, these designs are sure to become a family favorite; and here's the best part - they are so quick and easy to make that you will proudly say, "Yes, you can sit on this quilt.

Take it with you. Love it to pieces. When you wear it out, I'll make you a new one."

Happy Quilting!

Scotty & Friends - page 4

Scotty Dogs in a Row - page 9

Scotty & Red Dog
page 14

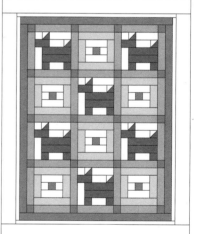

Scotty Dogs
Block by Block
page 18

Scotty & Favorite Things
page 10

Design Originals
For a color catalog featuring over 200 terrific 'How-To' books, **visit www.d-originals.com**

Scotty & Friends

There's no place like home! Scotty is barking at the butterflies and keeping clear of digging near the flower pots. The sun is shining and the house is ready for entertaining guests; or perhaps it's time to simply take it all in and relax on the porch steps.

This charming quilt holds all the sweetest reminiscences of enjoying life in your own back yard.

SIZE: 52" x 64"
YARDAGE:
We used a *Moda* "Jolly" by Mary Engelbreit 'Jelly Roll' collection of 2½" fabric strips
- we purchased 1 'Jelly Roll'

⅝ yard Black	OR	8 strips
⅝ yard Green	OR	8 strips
½ yard Golden Yellow	OR	6 strips
½ yard Red	OR	6 strips
⅔ yard White	OR	9 strips

Border #2	Purchase ¼ yard Red
Border #3 & Binding	Purchase 1⅝ yards Black
Backing	Purchase 4¼ yards
Batting	Purchase 60" x 72"

Sewing machine, needle, thread
DMC Black pearl cotton or 6-ply floss
#22 or #24 Chenille needle
3 Blue ⅞" buttons (not recommended for children)
1 White ⅜" button (not recommended for children)

Courthouse Steps – Red
BLOCK 3:
Black:

Quantity	Length	Position
1	2½"	Center - #2

White:

2	6½"	Center borders - #4, #5
2	2½"	Center - #1, #3

Red:

2	10½"	Border - #8, #9
2	6½"	Border - #6, #7

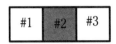

Center Row:
   Sew the following 2½" squares together:
      White - Black - White. Press.

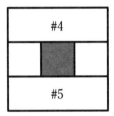

Add Top and Bottom Strips to the Center:
   Sew a White 6½" strip to the top and bottom of the piece. Press.

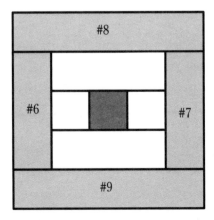

Add Surrounding Strips:
   Sew a Red 6½" strip to each side of the piece. Press.
   Sew a Red 10½" strip to the top and bottom. Press.

Courthouse Steps - Gold

BLOCKS 2, 4, 6, 8, 10, & 12:

Note: Quantity is for all 6 blocks.

Golden Yellow:

Quantity	Length	Position
12	10½"	Top & Bottom borders - #8, #9
12	6½"	Side borders - #6, #7

White:

2	15"	Center - #1, #2 (for 6 blocks)
12	6½"	Center borders - #4, #5

Red:

1	15"	Center - #2 (for 6 blocks)

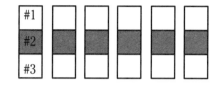

Speed Piece the Center:
Blocks 2, 4, 6, 8, 10, & 12

Sew the 15" strips together side by side to make a piece 6½" x 15": White - Red - White. Press.

Cut the piece into 6 units 2½" x 6½".

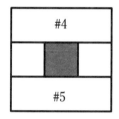

Add Top and Bottom Strips to the Center:

Sew a White 6½" strip to the top and bottom of each center unit. Press. Make 6.

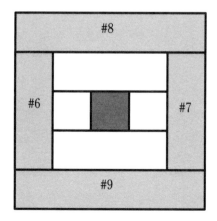

Add Surrounding Strips:

Sew a Yellow 6½" strip to the right and left sides. Press.

Sew a Yellow 10½" strip to the top and bottom. Press. Make 6.

Pinwheel Block

BLOCK 1:

Red:

Quantity	Length	Position
2	10½"	Top & Bottom borders - #7, #8
2	6½"	Side borders - #5, #6

Black:

2	9"	Pinwheel - #3, #4

White:

2	9"	Pinwheel - #1, #2

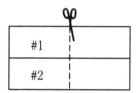 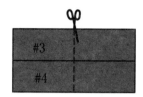

Make Squares for Pinwheels:

Sew 2 White 9" strips together side by side to make a strip 4½" x 9".

Sew 2 Black 9" strips together side by side to make a strip 4½" x 9".

Cut each strip into 2 squares 4½" x 4½".

Each pair of Black/White squares makes 2 Half-Square Triangle blocks

Half-Square Triangles:

TIP: Refer to diagram for Half-Square Triangle on page 15.

Pair up a Black square with a White square.

Draw a diagonal line from corner to corner.

Stitch ¼" on each side of the line.

Cut squares apart on the diagonal line.

Center and trim each square to 3½" x 3½".

Press. Make 4 Blocks.

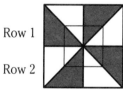

Row 1
Row 2

Pinwheel
Assembly Diagram

Pinwheels:

Refer to Pinwheel Assembly Diagram for color placement and direction of the diagonal.

Sew a row of 2 squares each. Press. Make 2.

Sew the 2 rows together.

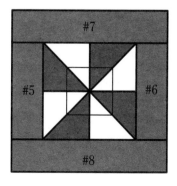

Add Surrounding Strips:

Sew a Red 6½" strip to each side. Press.

Sew a Red 10½" strip to the top and bottom. Press.

Butterfly Block

BLOCK 5:

Black:

Quantity	Length	Position
1	8½"	Center body

White:

7	2½"	Background

Red:

2	10½"	Side body
2	8½"	Wings
2	2½"	Wings

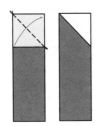 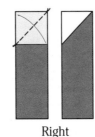

Left   Right

Connector Wing Strips:

Align a White 2½" square at the top of each
  Red 10½" strip.
Noting the direction of the diagonal, draw a diagonal
  line on each.
Sew on the diagonal line. Fold back the corner. Press.
Make 1 left and 1 right.
Trim excess fabric from underneath.

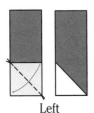 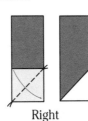

Left   Right

Top Outside Wings:

Align a White 2½" square at bottom of each
  Red 8½" strip.
Noting the direction of the diagonal, draw a diagonal
  line on each 2½" square.
Sew on the diagonal line.
Fold back the corner. Press.
Make 1 left and 1 right.
Trim excess fabric from underneath..

Left   Right

Bottom Outside Wings:

Align a White 2½" square with a Red 2½" square.
Noting the direction of the diagonal, draw a diagonal
  line on each 2½" square.
Sew on the diagonal line.
Fold back the corner. Press.
Make 1 left and 1 right.

Body:

Sew a White 2½"square to the top
of the Black 8½" center body strip.
Press.

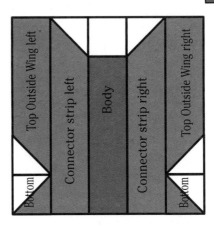

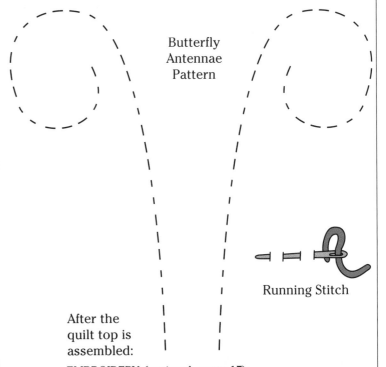

Assemble Outside Wing Strips:

Sew a Bottom Outside Wing to a Top Outside Wing.
  Press. Make 1 left and 1 right.

Assemble the Butterfly:

Sew a Connector strip to each side of the center
  Body strip. Press.
Sew an Outside Wing strip to each side. Press.

Butterfly
Antennae
Pattern

Running Stitch

After the
quilt top is
assembled:

EMBROIDERY (optional - page 17):
Use a water erasable marking pen or pencil (light lines) to
draw lines for antennae. Use 2-ply Pearl Cotton or 6-ply
Floss to make LONG Running Stitches needed for the
antennae. See Diagram.

House Block

BLOCK 7:

Black:

Quantity	Length	Position
1	10½"	Roof #7
1	6½"	Roof #6
1	4½"	Door #3
1	2½"	Window #1

Red:

1	10½"	Top of Wall #5
3	4½"	Walls #4
1	2½"	Wall #2

White:

6	2½"	Sky #8

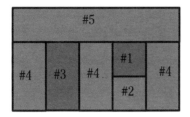

House Base:

Sew Black #1 and Red #2 squares together. Press.
Sew house walls together side by side:
  #4 - #3 - #4 - #1/2 - #4. Press.
Sew Red #5 to the top of the piece. Press.

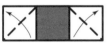 

Diagram A

Assemble the Roof:

Align a White #8 on each end of the Black #6.
Draw diagonal lines as shown.
Sew on the diagonal lines. Fold back the corners. Press.
Align a White #8 on each end of the Black #7.
Draw a diagonal line as shown in Diagram A.
Sew on the diagonal line. Fold back the corner. Press.
Trim excess fabric away from underneath.

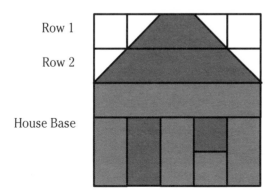

Row 1

Row 2

House Base

Assemble the House:

Sew Row 1 together: #8 - #6 - #8. Press.
Sew Row 1 and Row 2 together. Press.
Sew the roof to the house base. Press.

Flower Pot Block

BLOCK 11:

White:

Quantity	Length	Position
2	10½"	Side borders - #6, #7
3	6½"	Center top - #1, #2, #3

Red:

2	6½"	Flower pot - #4, #5

Top of Block:

Sew 3 White 6½" strips together side by side to make a piece 6½" x 6½". Press.

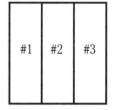

Flower Pot:

Sew 2 Red 6½" strips together side by side to make a piece 4½" x 6½". Press.

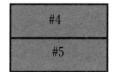

Assemble Block:

Sew the Top to the Flower Pot. Press.

Sew a White 10½" strip to each side of the piece. Press.

After the quilt is assembled APPLIQUE (optional): See page 17.

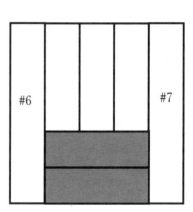

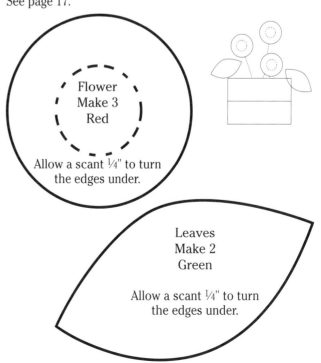

Flower
Make 3
Red

Allow a scant ¼" to turn the edges under.

Leaves
Make 2
Green

Allow a scant ¼" to turn the edges under.

Scotty Dog Block

BLOCK 9:

Black:

Quantity	Length	Position
2	8½"	Body
1	4½"	Head
4	2½"	Legs, Ear, Tail

White:

3	6½"	Sky
2	4½"	Sky

Body: Sew 2 Black 8½" strips together side by side to make a piece 4½" x 8½". Press.

Feet: Sew a Black 2½" square to each end of a White 4½" strip to make a piece 2½" x 8½". Press.

Head and Tail:

Ears:
Align a Black 2½" square with the end of a White 4½" strip.

Tail:
Align a Black 2½" square with the end of a White 6½" strip.
Draw a diagonal line on each.
Sew on the diagonal line.
Fold back the corner. Press.
Trim excess fabric from underneath.

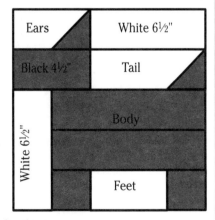

Assemble the Body Section:
Sew the Body to the Feet. Press.
Sew a White 6½" strip to the left side. Press.

Assemble the Head Section:
Row 1: Sew Ears section to a White 6½" strip. Press.
Row 2: Sew a Black 4½" strip to the Tail section. Press.
Sew Row 1 and Row 2 together side by side. Press.

Assemble the Dog:
Sew the Head Section to the Body section. Press.

Each block will measure 10½" x 10½" at this point.

Sashing Strips & Cornerstones:
Cut 31 Green 10½" sashing strips. Cut 20 White 2½" squares.

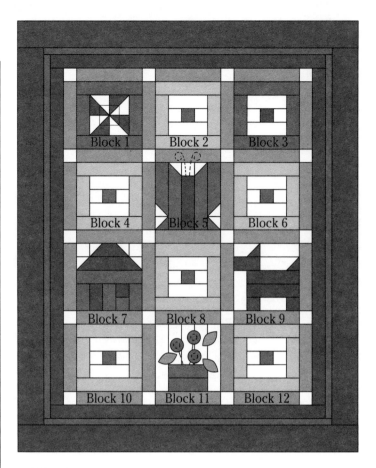

ASSEMBLY:
Arrange all Blocks and strips on a work surface or table. Refer to the diagram for block placement and direction. Sew the pieces together in 4 rows, 3 blocks per row. Press. Sew rows together. Press.

APPLIQUE & EMBROIDERY (optional):
Applique flowers and leaves. Embroider the flower stems and butterfly antennae.

Pieced Border #1:
Sew 5 Black strips together end to end.
Cut 2 strips 2½" x 50½" for sides.
Cut 2 strips 2½" x 42½" for top and bottom.
Sew side borders to the quilt. Press.
Sew top and bottom borders to the quilt. Press.

Red Border #2:
Cut six 1½" strips by the width of fabric.
Sew strips together end to end.
Cut 2 strips 1½" x 54½" for sides.
Cut 2 strips 1½" x 44½" for top and bottom.
Sew side borders to the quilt. Press.
Sew top and bottom borders to the quilt. Press.

Black Border #3:
Cut strips 4½" wide parallel to the selvage to prevent piecing.
Cut 2 strips 4½" x 56½" for sides.
Cut 2 strips 4½" x 52½" for top and bottom.
Sew side borders to the quilt. Press.
Sew top and bottom borders to the quilt. Press.

FINISHING:
Quilting: See Basic Instructions on pages 15 - 17.
Binding: Cut strips 2½" wide.
Sew together end to end to equal 242".
See Binding Instructions on page 17.

Buttons: Sew buttons on Flowers and Scotty.
NOTE: Do not use buttons on quilts intended for babies and toddlers. Embroider accents with floss.

Scotty Dogs in a Row
Variation Quilt

These happy Scotty dogs stand ready to welcome your baby to the nursery. Best of all, this design will still be welcome when your child sets aside the "baby stuff" and moves to the first child-size bed.

SIZE: 44" x 52"

YARDAGE:
We used a *Moda* "Jolly" by Mary Engelbreit
'Jelly Roll' collection of 2½" fabric strips
- we purchased 1 'Jelly Roll'

⅜ yard Black	OR	5 strips
⅓ yard Green	OR	4 strips
⅛ yard Golden Yellow	OR	1 strip
⅓ yard Red	OR	4 strips
½ yard White	OR	7 strips

Border #1	Purchase ½ yard Black
Border #2	Purchase ¼ yards Red
Border #3 & Binding	Purchase 1⅓ yards Black
Backing	Purchase 2⅛ yards
Batting	Purchase 52" x 60"

Sewing machine, needle, thread
6 White ⅜" buttons (not recommended for children)

SCOTTY DOG BLOCKS:
Refer to the Scotty Dog block instructions on page 8.
    Cut and make 4 Scotty Dogs facing left (for rows 1 and 3).
    Cut and make 2 Scotty Dogs facing right (for row 2), see variation.

SASHING STRIPS & CORNERSTONES:
  Strips: Cut 9 White 10½", 6 Green 10½", 8 Green 12½".
  Squares: Cut 12 Gold 2½" squares for cornerstones.

Scotty Dog Block Variation – (Right)

Refer to the pattern on page 8.
Cut out the same amount of pieces. Make a Body and Feet.

Ears:
Align a Black 2½" and White 4½" strips.
Tail:
Align a Black 2½" and White 6½" strip.
    Draw a diagonal line on each.
    Sew on the diagonal line.
    Fold back the corner. Press.

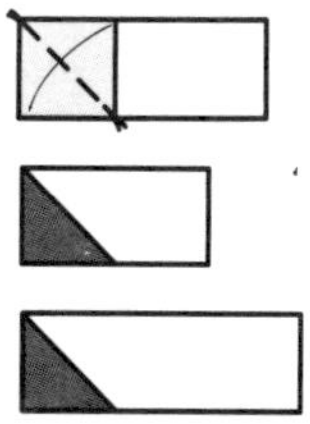

Assemble Dog:
Refer to the diagram to make a Scotty facing right. Sew the pieces together.
Press.

ASSEMBLY:
    Arrange blocks, strips, and squares on a work surface or table.
    Refer to diagram for block placement and direction.
    Sew each Sashing row in the following order:
        Gold 2½" - Green 12½" - Gold 2½" - Green 12½" - Gold 2½".
        Make 4 Sashing rows. Press.
    Sew each Scotty Dog row in the following order:
        Green 10½"- White 10½" - Dog - White 10½" -
            Dog - White 10½" - Green 10½".
        Make 3 Scotty Dog rows. Press.
    Sew rows together in the following order:
        Sashing - Row 1 - Sashing - Row 2 - Sashing - Row 3 - Sashing.
        Press.

Black Border #1:
    Cut 2 strips 2½" x 38½" for sides.
    Cut 2 strips 2½" x 34½" for top and bottom.
    Sew side borders to the quilt. Press.
    Sew top and bottom borders to the quilt. Press.

Red Border #2:
Cut four 1½" wide strips by the width of fabric.
    Cut 2 strips 1½" x 42½" for sides.
    Cut 2 strips 1½" x 36½" for top and bottom.
    Sew side borders to the quilt. Press.
    Sew top and bottom borders to the quilt. Press.

Black Border #3:
Cut 4½" wide strips parallel to the selvage to eliminate piecing.
    Cut 2 strips 4½" x 44½" for sides.
    Cut 2 strips 4½" x 44½" for top and bottom.
    Sew side borders to the quilt. Press.
    Sew top and bottom borders to the quilt. Press.

FINISHING:
Quilting: See Basic Instructions on pages 15 - 17.
Binding: Cut strips 2½" wide.
            Sew together end to end to equal 202".
            See Binding Instructions on page 17.

After quilting and binding,
    sew a button on each Scotty for an eye.
    NOTE: Do not use buttons on quilts intended for babies and young children.
    Embroider an eye with White floss.

Scotty & Favorite Things

Simple shapes enliven the solid squares while half-square triangle blocks add variety, color and movement to the design on this attractive quilt.

Perfect for a beginner, this project provides a great opportunity to practice basic applique and embroidery techniques as well as simple piecing skills.

SIZE: 57" x 66"

YARDAGE:
We used a *Moda* "Jolly" by Mary Engelbreit collection of 'Layer Cake' 10" x 10" fabric squares
- we purchased 1 Layer Cake Pack of 10" fabric squares
(You'll need a total of 39 squares 10" x 10")

13 White	OR	1⅛ yard
7 Black	OR	⅝ yard
8 Green	OR	⅝ yard
6 Red	OR	⅝ yard
5 Golden Yellow	OR	⅝ yard

Border #1	Purchase ¼ yard Green
Border #2	Purchase ¼ yards Red
Border #3	Purchase 2 yards White print
Binding	Purchase ½ yard Green
Backing	Purchase 4¼ yards
Batting	Purchase 65" x 74"

Sewing machine, needle, thread
DMC Black pearl cotton or 6-ply floss
#22 or #24 Chenille needle
2 White ⅜" buttons (not recommended for children)

SORTING:
Set aside the following 10" x 10" squares for appliques:
    3 White
    2 Red
    2 Black
    1 Green

Set aside the following 10" x 10" squares, trim to 9½" x 9½":
    10 White
    5 Golden Yellow

Set aside the following 10" x 10" squares to make half-square triangles:
    4 Red
    7 Green
    5 Black

HALF-SQUARE TRIANGLES:
Half-Square Triangles:
TIP: Refer to diagram for Half-Square Triangle on page 15.

Pair up the following squares for the half-square triangles:
    3 pairs of Green-Red
    4 pairs of Green-Black
    1 pair of Black-Red

Draw a diagonal line from corner to corner.
    Stitch ¼" on each side of the line.
    Cut squares apart on the diagonal line.
    Center and trim each square to 9½" x 9½".
    Press.
    Make a total of 16 half-square triangles
        (you'll have 1 leftover).

ASSEMBLY:
    Arrange all Blocks on a work surface or table.
    Refer to diagram for block placement and direction.
    Sew blocks together in 6 rows, 5 blocks per row. Press.
    Sew rows together. Press.

Green Border #1:
Cut five 1½" strips the width of fabric.
Sew strips together end to end.
    Cut 2 strips 1½" x 54½" for sides.
    Cut 2 strips 1½" x 47½" for top and bottom.
    Sew side borders to the quilt. Press.
    Sew top and bottom borders to the quilt.
    Press.

Red Border #2:
Cut five 1½" strips the width of fabric.
Sew strips together end to end.
    Cut 2 strips 1½" x 56½" for sides.
    Cut 2 strips 1½" x 49½" for top and bottom.
    Sew side borders to the quilt. Press.
    Sew top and bottom borders to the quilt.
    Press.

White Border #3:
Cut strips 4½" wide
    (or adjust to fit a repeat when you use a
    stripe on your fabric).
NOTE: Cut strips parallel to the selvage to
    eliminate piecing.
For a Mitered Border:
    Cut 2 strips 4½" x 68½" for sides.
    Cut 2 strips 4½" x 59½" for top and bottom.
    Center the borders leaving 4½" on each end
        to allow for mitering.
    Sew borders to the quilt, mitering the
        corners (see illustrations). Press.

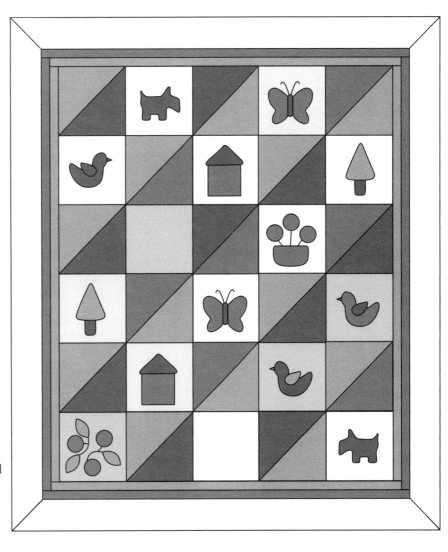

FINISHING:
Quilting:
    See Basic Instructions on pages 15 - 17.
Binding:
    Cut strips 2½" wide on the crosswise grain.
    Sew together end to end to equal 256".
    See Binding Instructions on page 17.
After quilting and binding,
    sew a button on each Scotty for an eye.
    NOTE: Do not use buttons on quilts
    intended for babies and young children.
    Embroider an eye with White floss.

APPLIQUE (optional):
    See Applique and Embroidery instructions on page 17.
    Use the desired method of applique.
    Use the applique patterns on pages 12 - 13
    Position designs on each block as desired.
    Applique them in place.

EMBROIDERY (optional):
    Use a water erasable marking pen or pencil (light lines) to draw
        lines for Butterfly antennae and Flower stems.
    Use 2-ply Pearl Cotton or 6-ply Embroidery Floss to make
        LONG Running Stitches as accents to the applique.

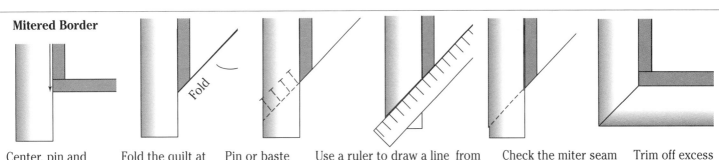

Mitered Border

Center, pin and sew borders to the sides of the quilt. Stop the seam at the corner.

Fold the quilt at a diagonal so the miter will extend from the corner outward.

Pin or baste miter seam, carefully, lining up the pattern.

Use a ruler to draw a line from the corner out to the edge of the border. Sew a seam.
TIP: I use a long stitch in case I need to rip it out and redo it.

Check the miter seam to be sure it lines up correctly and lays down flat, resew it with a normal stitch.

Trim off excess fabric underneath the corners. Repeat on all 4 corners.

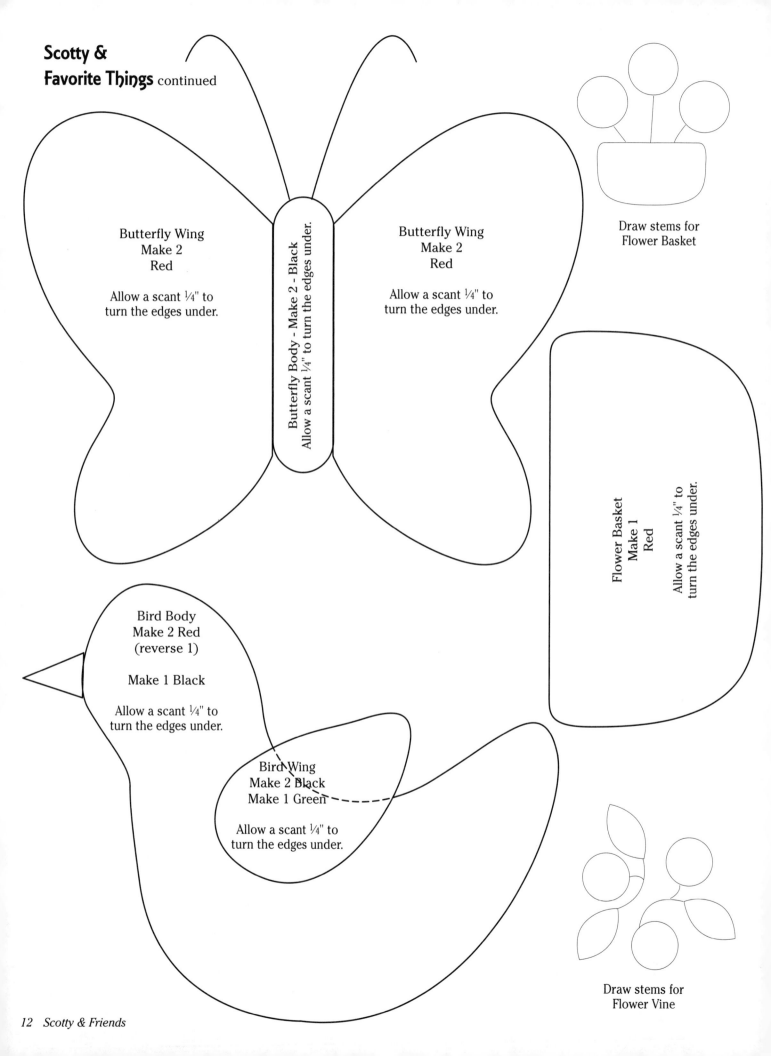

Butterfly Wing
Make 2
Red

Allow a scant ¼" to
turn the edges under.

Butterfly Body - Make 2 - Black
Allow a scant ¼" to turn the edges under.

Butterfly Wing
Make 2
Red

Allow a scant ¼" to
turn the edges under.

Draw stems for
Flower Basket

Flower Basket
Make 1
Red

Allow a scant ¼" to
turn the edges under.

Bird Body
Make 2 Red
(reverse 1)

Make 1 Black

Allow a scant ¼" to
turn the edges under.

Bird Wing
Make 2 Black
Make 1 Green

Allow a scant ¼" to
turn the edges under.

Draw stems for
Flower Vine

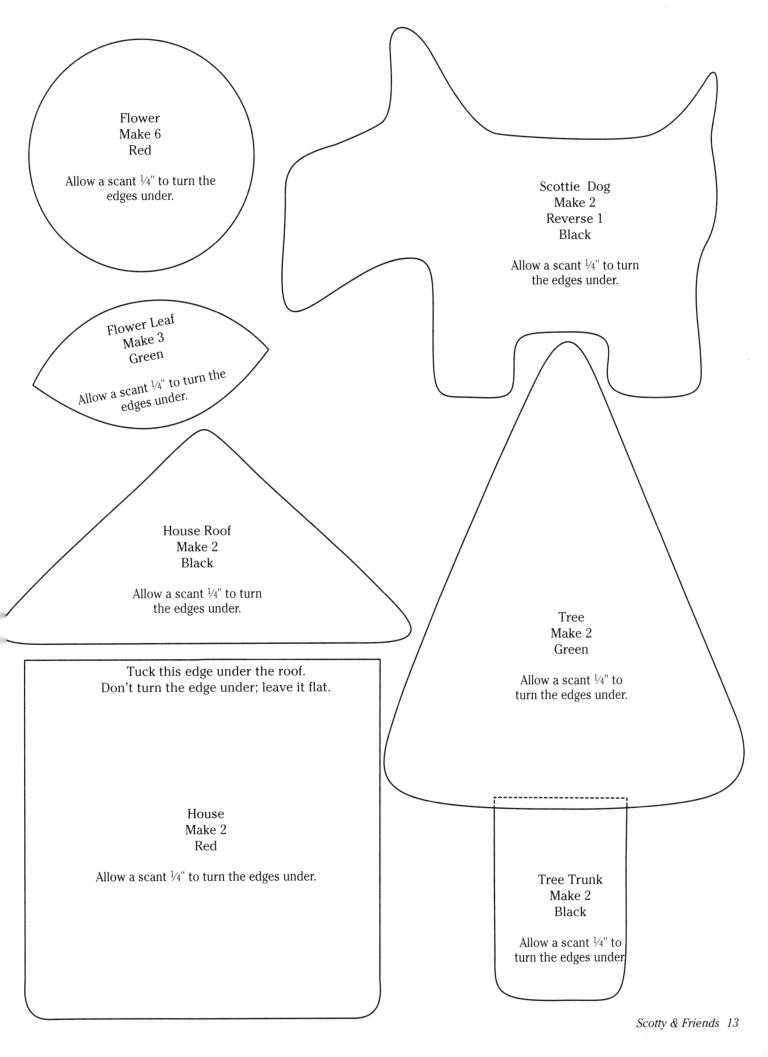

Flower
Make 6
Red

Allow a scant ¼" to turn the
edges under.

Scottie Dog
Make 2
Reverse 1
Black

Allow a scant ¼" to turn
the edges under.

Flower Leaf
Make 3
Green

Allow a scant ¼" to turn the
edges under.

House Roof
Make 2
Black

Allow a scant ¼" to turn
the edges under.

Tree
Make 2
Green

Allow a scant ¼" to
turn the edges under.

Tuck this edge under the roof.
Don't turn the edge under; leave it flat.

House
Make 2
Red

Allow a scant ¼" to turn the edges under.

Tree Trunk
Make 2
Black

Allow a scant ¼" to
turn the edges under

Scotty & Red Dog
Variation

Happiness is a warm puppy quilt! This very comfortable size lap quilt is perfect for the dog lover in your family, especially those who hold dogs most dear.

Facing both directions, these dogs are on the lookout for Clifford, the red dog.

SIZE: 48" x 66"
YARDAGE:
We used a *Moda* "Jolly" by Mary Engelbreit collection of 'Layer Cake' 10" x 10" squares
- we purchased 1 Layer Cake Pack of 10" fabric squares
(You'll need a total of 31 squares 10" x 10")

8 White	OR	⅝ yard
8 Black	OR	⅝ yard
6 Green	OR	⅝ yard
5 Red	OR	⅝ yard
4 Golden Yellow	OR	⅓ yard

Border #1	Purchase ¼ yard Green
Border #2	Purchase ¼ yard Red
Border #3	Purchase 1⅝ yards White print
Binding	Purchase ½ yard Green
Backing	Purchase 3⅛ yards
Batting	Purchase 56" x 74"

Sewing machine, needle, thread
12 White ⅜" buttons (not recommended for children)

SORTING:
Set aside the following 10" x 10" squares for appliques:
  1 Red
  4 Black
Set aside the following 10" x 10" squares and trim to 9½" x 9½":
  8 White
  4 Golden Yellow
Set aside the following 10" x 10" squares to make half-square triangles:
  4 Red
  6 Green
  4 Black

Half-Square Triangles:
TIP: Refer to diagram for Half-Square Triangle on page 15.
Pair up the following squares for the half-square triangles:
  3 pairs of Green-Red
  3 pairs of Green-Black
  1 pair of Black-Red
Draw a diagonal line from corner to corner.
  Stitch ¼" on each side of the line.
  Cut squares apart on the diagonal line.
  Center and trim each square to 9½" x 9½". Press.
  Make a total of 12 half-square triangles.

ASSEMBLY:
  Arrange Blocks on a work surface or table. Refer to diagram.
  Sew blocks together in 6 rows, 4 blocks per row. Press.
  Sew rows together. Press.

Green Border #1:
Cut five 1½" wide strips by the width of fabric.
Sew strips together end to end.
  Cut 2 strips 1½" x 54½" for sides.
  Cut 2 strips 1½" x 38½" for top and bottom.
  Sew borders to the quilt. Press.

Red Border #2:
Cut five 1½" wide strips by the width of fabric.
Sew strips together end to end.
  Cut 2 strips 1½" x 56½" for sides.
  Cut 2 strips 1½" x 40½" for top and bottom.
  Sew borders to the quilt. Press.

White Border #3:
Cut strips 4½" wide or adjust to fit the repeat on the fabric.
Cut strips parallel to the selvage to eliminate piecing.
  Cut 2 strips 4½" x 68½" for sides.
  Cut 2 strips 4½" x 50½" for top and bottom.
  For Mitered Borders, see page 11.

FINISHING:
Quilting:
  See Basic Instructions on pages 15 - 17.
Binding:
  Cut strips 2½" wide.
  Sew together end to end to equal 238".
  See Binding Instructions on page 17.
After quilting and binding, sew a button on each Scotty for an eye.
  NOTE: Do not use buttons on quilts intended for babies and young children. Embroider an eye with White floss.

APPLIQUE (optional):
  Follow the Applique Instructions on page 17.
  Make the following Scotty Dogs (pattern on page 13):
    5 Black dogs facing right
    6 Black dogs facing left
    1 Red dog facing left

Basic Quilting Instructions

Hand Quilting:

Many quilters enjoy the serenity of hand quilting. Because the quilt is handled a great deal, it is important to securely baste the sandwich together. Place the quilt in a hoop and don't forget to hide your knots.

Machine Quilting:

All the quilts in this book were machine quilted. Some were quilted on a large, free-arm quilting machine and others were quilted on a sewing machine. If you have never machine quilted before, practice on some scraps first.

Straight Line Machine Quilting Tips:

1. Pin baste the layers securely.

2. Set up your sewing machine with a size 80 quilting needle and a walking foot.

3. Experimenting with the decorative stitches on your machine adds interest to your quilt. You do not have to quilt the entire piece with the same stitch. Variety is the spice of life, so have fun trying out stitches you have never used before as well as your favorite stand-bys.

Free Motion Machine Quilting Tips:

1. Pin baste the layers securely.

2. Set up your sewing machine with a spring needle, a quilting foot, and lower the feed dogs.

Basic Mitered Binding Instructions

A Perfect Finish:

The binding endures the most stress on a quilt and is usually the first thing to wear out. For this reason, we recommend using a double fold binding.

1. Trim the backing and batting even with the quilt edge.

2. If possible cut strips on the crosswise grain because a little bias in the binding is a Good thing. This is the only place in the quilt where bias is helpful, for it allows the binding to give as it is turned to the back and sewn in place.

3. Strips are usually cut 2½" wide, but check the instructions for your project before cutting.

4. Sew strips end to end to make a long strip sufficient to go all around the quilt plus 4"- 6".

5. With wrong sides together, fold the strip in half lengthwise. Press.

6. Stretch out your hand and place your little finger at the corner of the quilt top. Place the binding where your thumb touches the edge of the quilt. Aligning the edge of the quilt with the raw edges of the binding, pin the binding in place along the first side.

7. Leaving a 2" tail for later use, begin sewing the binding to the quilt with a ¼" seam.

For Mitered Corners:

1. Stop ¼" from the first corner. Leave the needle in the quilt and turn it 90°. Hit the reverse button on your machine and back off the quilt leaving the threads connected.

2. Fold the binding perpendicular to the side you sewed, making a 45° angle. Carefully maintaining the first fold, bring the binding back along the edge to be sewn.

3. Carefully align the edges of the binding with the quilt edge and sew as you did the first side. Repeat this process until you reach the tail left at the beginning. Fold the tail out of the way and sew until you are ¼" from the beginning stitches.

4. Remove the quilt from the machine. Fold the quilt out of the way and match the binding tails together. Carefully sew the binding tails with a ¼" seam. You can do this by hand if you prefer.

Finishing the Binding:

5. Trim the seam to reduce bulk.

6. Finish stitching the binding to the quilt across the join you just sewed.

7. Turn the binding to the back of the quilt. To reduce bulk at the corners, fold the miter in the opposite direction from which it was folded on the front.

8. Hand-sew a Blind stitch on the back of the quilt to secure the binding in place.

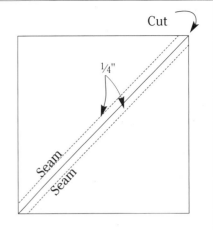

Half-Square Triangle Diagram
1. Place 2 squares right sides together.
2. Draw a diagonal line from corner to corner.
3. Stitch ¼" on each side of the line.
4. Cut squares apart on the diagonal line.
5. Open the 2 new squares with 2 colors.
6. Press. Trim off dog-ears.
7. Center and trim to size.

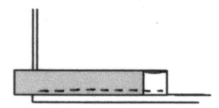

Align the raw edge of the binding with the raw edge of the quilt top. Start about 8" from the corner and go along the first side with a ¼" seam.

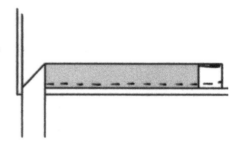

Stop ¼" from the edge. Then stitch a slant to the corner (through both layers of binding)... lift up, then down, as you line up the edge. Fold the binding back.

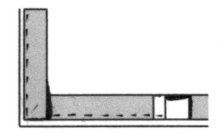

Align the raw edge again. Continue stitching the next side with a ¼" seam as you sew the binding in place.

Tips for Working with Strips and Squares

TIPS: As a Guide for Yardage:

Each 1/4 yard or a 'Fat Quarter' equals 3 strips

A pre-cut 'Jelly Roll' strip is $2^1/2$" x 44"

Cut 'Fat Quarter' strips to $2^1/2$" x 22"

Pre-cut strips and squares are often cut on the crosswise grain and are prone to stretching. These tips will help reduce stretching and make your quilt lay flat for quilting.

1. If you are cutting yardage, cut on the grain. Cut fat quarters on grain, parallel to the 18" side.

2. When sewing crosswise grain strips together, take care not to stretch the strips. If you detect any puckering as you go, rip out the seam and sew it again.

3. Press, Do Not Iron. Carefully open fabric, with the seam to one side, press without moving the iron. A back-and-forth ironing motion stretches the fabric.

4. Reduce the wiggle in your borders with this technique from garment making. First, accurately cut your borders to the exact measure of the quilt top. Then, before sewing the border to the quilt, run a double row of stay stitches along the outside edge to maintain the original shape and prevent stretching. Pin the border to the quilt, taking care not to stretch the quilt top to make it fit. Pinning reduces slipping and stretching.

Rotary Cutting Tips

Rotary Cutter: Friend or Foe

A rotary cutter is wonderful and useful. When not used correctly, the sharp blade can be a dangerous tool. Follow these safety tips:

1. Never cut toward you.

2. Use a sharp blade. Pressing harder on a dull blade can cause the blade to jump the ruler and injure your fingers.

3. Always disengage the blade before the cutter leaves your hand, even if you intend to pick it up immediately.

Rotary cutters have been caught when lifting fabric, have fallen onto the floor and have cut fingers.

Basic Sewing Instructions

You now have precisely cut strips that are exactly the correct width. You are well on your way to blocks that fit together perfectly. Accurate sewing is the next important step.

Matching Edges:

1. Carefully line up the edges of your strips. Many times, if the underside is off a little, your seam will be off by 1/8". This does not sound like much until you have 8 seams in a block, each off by 1/8". Now your finished block is a whole inch wrong!

2. Pin the pieces together to prevent them shifting.

Seam Allowance:

I cannot stress enough the importance of accurate 1/4" seams. All the quilts in this book are measured for 1/4" seams unless otherwise indicated.

Most sewing machine manufacturers offer a Quarter-inch foot. A Quarter-inch foot is the most worthwhile investment you can make in your quilting.

Pressing:

I want to talk about pressing even before we get to sewing because proper pressing can make the difference between a quilt that wins a ribbon at the quilt show and one that does not.

Press, do NOT iron. What does that mean? Many of us want to move the iron back and forth along the seam. This "ironing" stretches the strip out of shape and creates errors that accumulate as the quilt is constructed. Believe it or not, there is a correct way to press your seams, and here it is:

1. Do NOT use steam with your iron. If you need a little water, spritz it on.

2. Place your fabric flat on the ironing board without opening the seam. Set a hot iron on the seam and count to 3. Lift the iron and move to the next position along the seam. Repeat until the entire seam is pressed. This sets and sinks the threads into the fabric.

3. Now, carefully lift the top strip and fold it away from you so the seam is on one side. Usually the seam is pressed toward the darker fabric, but often the direction of the seam is determined by the piecing requirements.

4. Press the seam open with your fingers. Add a little water or spray starch if it wants to close again. Lift the iron and place it on the seam. Count to 3. Lift the iron again and continue until the seam is pressed. Do NOT use the tip of the iron to push the seam open. So many people do this and wonder later why their blocks are not fitting together.

5. Most critical of all: For accuracy every seam must be pressed before the next seam is sewn.

Working with 'Crosswise Grain' strips:

Strips cut on the crosswise grain (from selvage to selvage) have problems similar to bias edges and are prone to stretching. To reduce stretching and make your quilt lay flat for quilting, keep these tips in mind.

1. Take care not to stretch the strips as you sew.

2. Adjust the sewing thread tension and the presser foot pressure if needed.

3. If you detect any puckering as you go, rip out the seam and sew it again. It is easier to take out a seam now than after the block is sewn.

Sewing Bias Edges:

Bias edges wiggle and stretch out of shape very easily. They are not recommended for beginners, but even a novice can accomplish bias edges if these techniques are employed.

1. Stabilize the bias edge with one of these methods:

    a) Press with spray starch.

    b) Press freezer paper or removable iron-on stabilizer to the back of the fabric.

    c) Sew a double row of stay stitches along the bias edge and ⅛" from the bias edge. This is a favorite technique of garment makers.

2. Pin, pin, pin! I know many of us dislike pinning, but when working with bias edges, pinning makes the difference between intersections that match and those that do not.

Building Better Borders:

Wiggly borders make a quilt very difficult to finish. However, wiggly borders can be avoided with these techniques.

1. Cut the borders on grain. That means cutting your strips parallel to the selvage edge.

2. Accurately cut your borders to the exact measure of the quilt.

3. If your borders are piece stripped from crosswise grain fabrics, press well with spray starch and sew a double row of stay stitches along the outside edge to maintain the original shape and prevent stretching.

4. Pin the border to the quilt, taking care not to stretch the quilt top to make it fit. Pinning reduces slipping and stretching.

Embroidery Use 24" lengths of doubled pearl cotton or 6-ply floss and a #22 or #24 Chenille needle (this needle has a large eye). Outline large elements.

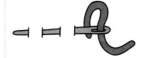

Running Stitch Come up at A. Weave the needle through the fabric, making LONG stitches on the top and SHORT stitches on the bottom. Keep stitches even.

Basic Layering Instructions

Marking Your Quilt:

If you choose to mark your quilt for hand or machine quilting, it is much easier to do so before layering. Press your quilt before you begin. Here are some handy tips regarding marking.

1. A disappearing pen may vanish before you finish.

2. Use a White pencil on dark fabrics.

3. If using a washable Blue pen, remember that pressing may make the pen permanent.

Pieced Backings:

1. Press the backing fabric before measuring.

2. If possible cut backing fabrics on grain, parallel to the selvage edges.

3. Piece 3 parts rather than 2 whenever possible, sewing 2 side borders to the center. This reduces stress on the pieced seam.

4. The backing and batting should extend at least 2" on each side of the quilt.

Creating a Quilt Sandwich:

1. Press the backing and top to remove all wrinkles.

2. Lay the backing wrong side up on the table.

3. Position the batting over the backing and smooth out all wrinkles.

4. Center the quilt top over the batting leaving a 2" border all around.

5. Pin the layers together with 2" safety pins positioned a handwidth apart. A grapefruit spoon makes inserting the pins easier. Leaving the pins open in the container speeds up the basting on the next quilt.

Applique Instructions

Basic Turned Edge:

1. Trace pattern onto template plastic.

2. Cut out the shape leaving a scant ¼" fabric border all around and clip the curves.

3. Place the template plastic on the wrong side of the fabric. Spray edges with starch.

4. Press the ⅛" border over the edge of the template plastic with the tip of a hot iron. Press firmly.

5. Remove the template, maintaining the folded edge on the back of the fabric.

6. Position the shape on the quilt and Blindstitch in place.

Basic Needle Turn:

1. Cut out the shape leaving a ¼" fabric border all around.

2. Baste the shapes to the quilt, keeping the basting stitches away from the edge of the fabric.

3. Begin with all areas that are under other layers and work to the topmost layer.

4. For an area no more than 2" ahead of where you are working, trim to ⅛" and clip the curves.

5. Using the needle, roll the edge under and sew tiny Blindstitches to secure.

Using Fusible Web for Iron-on Applique:

1. Trace the pattern onto *Steam a Seam 2* fusible web.

2. Press the patterns onto the wrong side of the fabric.

3. Cut out patterns exactly on the drawn line.

4. Score the web paper with a pin, then remove the paper.

5. Position the fabric, fusible side down, on the quilt. Press with a hot iron following the fusible web manufacturer's instructions.

6. Stitch around the edge by hand.

Optional: Stabilize the wrong side of the fabric with your favorite stabilizer.

Use a size 80 machine embroidery needle. Fill the bobbin with lightweight basting thread and thread the machine with a machine embroidery thread that complements the color being appliqued.

Set your machine for a Zigzag stitch and adjust the thread tension if needed. Use a scrap to experiment with different stitch widths and lengths until you find the one you like best.

Sew slowly.

SIZE: 52" x 64"

YARDAGE:
We used a *Moda* "Jolly" by Mary Engelbreit
'Jelly Roll' collection of 2½" fabric strips
- we purchased 1 'Jelly Roll'

⅜ yard Black	OR	5 strips
⅝ yard Green	OR	8 strips
½ yard Golden Yellow	OR	6 strips
⅙ yard Red	OR	2 strips
½ yard White	OR	7 strips

Border #1   Purchase ½ yard Black
Border #2   Purchase ¼ yard Red
Border #3 & Binding   Purchase 1⅝ yards Black
Backing   Purchase 4¼ yards
Batting   Purchase 60" x 72"

Sewing machine, needle, thread
6 White ⅜" buttons (not recommended for children)

MAKING THE BLOCKS:
    Follow the instructions for the
        Courthouse Steps - Gold blocks on page 5.
        Make 6.
    Follow the instructions for the
        Scotty Dog block on page 8.
        Make 6.

SASHING STRIPS & CORNERSTONES:
    Cut 31 Green 10½" sashing strips.
    Cut 20 Red 2½" squares for cornerstones.

ASSEMBLY:
TIP: Complete the quilt in the same manner as
        the Scotty & Friends quilt on pages 4 - 8.
Alternate the Scotty Dog blocks and
        Courthouse Steps blocks as shown.
Add all Borders.
    Note: Border #1 is cut from purchased
    fabric and does not need to be pieced.
After quilting and binding,
        sew a button on each Scotty for an eye.
    NOTE: Do not use buttons on quilts
    intended for babies and young children.
    Embroider an eye with White floss.

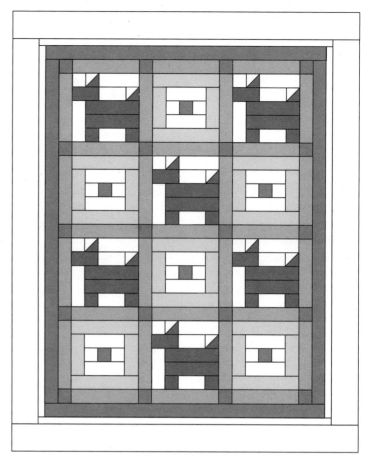

Scotty Dogs
Block by Block
Variation Quilt

Nothing will ever match the comfort we receive from the family dogs. Celebrate your regard for our furry friends with a delightful pack of Scotties brought to life on this wonderful quilt.

These are all standing at attention, tails wagging and ready for adventure, even if it is only a walk in the park.

The Best Things About Jelly Rolls & Layer Cakes

Non-Fattening • Sugar Free • No Cholesterol

Basic Instructions for Cutting, Sewing,
Layering, Quilting and Binding are
on pages 15 - 17.

TIPS: As a Guide for Yardage:
Each ¼ yard or a 'Fat Quarter' equals 3 strips.
A pre-cut 'Jelly Roll' strip is 2½" x 44".
Cut 'Fat Quarter' and yardage strips to 2½" x 20".

Yardage is given for using either
'Jelly Roll' strips or fabric yardage.

Supplier - Most quilt and fabric stores carry an excellent assortment of supplies. If you need something special, ask your local store to contact the following companies.

FABRICS, 'JELLY ROLLS', 'FAT QUARTERS'
   Moda and United Notions, Dallas, TX, 972-484-8901

QUILTER
   Sue Needle, 817-589-1168

MANY THANKS to my staff for their cheerful help and wonderful ideas!
    Kathy Mason • Patty Williams • Janet Long • David & Donna Thomason
Donna Kinsey for skillfully and patiently editing the instructions in this book